BOKER TOV
LAILAH TOV

Days of Wonder Nights of Peace

FAMILY PRAYERS IN SONG FOR MORNING AND BEDTIME

BY MAH TOVU

BEHRMAN HOUSE, INC.

MODEH ANI

Words and Music by Mah Tovu
(Brodsky, Chasen, and Zweiback)
©1998.
Produced and arranged by
Gordon Lustig.
Acoustic guitars/Synth: Gordon Lustig
Electric Guitars: Craig Stull
Bass: John Hatton
Drums: Bill Severance
Trumpets: Roy Weigans Jr.
Trombones: Bob McChesney
Saxes: Brian Scanlan
Recorded at JoMusik Studio,
Joe Milton, Engineer;
Max-O Music, Gordon Lustig, Engineer.
Mastered by Danny McKinney,
Requisite Masters.

ROUND AND ROUND

Words and Music by Mah Tovu
(Brodsky, Chasen, and Zweiback)
©1997.
Produced and Arranged by
Gordon Lustig.
Acoustic guitars: Gordon Lustig
Electric Guitars: Tom Bethke
Electric Bass: Ron Sures
Drums: Jeff Stern
Piano: Wally Minko
Fiddle: Candy Lerman
Pedal Steel: Doug Livingston
Recorded at The Track House,
John Ugarte, Engineer;
Lincoln Logs Cabin,
Lincoln Schleifer, Engineer;
The Rainbow Garage,
Rick Cunha, Engineer.
Additional recording at
Doug Messinger's,
Doug Messinger, Engineer.

THANK YOU GOD

Words and music by Mah Tovu
(Brodsky, Chasen, and Zweiback)
©2000.
Produced and arranged by
Gordon Lustig.
Acoustic guitars/synth: Gordon Lustig
Fretless Bass: Kevin Axt
Flutes: Tom Evans
Percussion: Scott Breadman
Recorded at The Rainbow Garage,
Rick Cunha, Engineer;
Max-O-Music, Gordon Lustig, Engineer.

HASHKIVEINU

Music by Mah Tovu
(Brodsky, Chasen, Zweiback) ©1990.
"Shelter Us" words and music ©
Larry Jonas.
Produced and Arranged by Sam Glaser.
Executive produced by Mah Tovu.
Acoustic Guitar: Steve Brodsky
Piano, keyboards: Sam Glaser
Bass: Larry Steen
Cello: Harry Gilbert
Background vocals: Michael Ian Elias,
Ramiro Fauve, Michel Turner, C.C. White
Recorded at Glaser MusicWorks,
Sam Glaser, Engineer.
Mastered by Doug Doyle, Digital Bros.

Mixed at The Rainbow Garage.
Remastered at Audio Mechanics by
John Polito.

To contact Mah Tovu, e-mail
mahtovu@aol.com

Modeh Ani, Yotzeir Or, Modim,
Hashkiveinu prayers and the Sh'ma
from traditional liturgy.
Safta Bishlah Daisah from traditional
Israeli nursery rhyme.

Project Editor: Vicki L. Weber
Book, Cover, and CD Design: O'Grady Ramá Design
Cover Art: Susan Shoshana Ramá
Cover Photo: Deborah Snyder

Copyright © 2001 Behrman House, Inc.
ISBN 0-87441-724-4
Published by Behrman House, Inc. www.behrmanhouse.com/family

Manufactured in the United States of America

INTRODUCTION

 *IMAGINE THE WORLD OF OUR ANCESTORS. The setting of the sun brought utter darkness, unbroken by the comfort of electric lights. The working day was fixed by the hours of available sunlight, and life was closely linked to the rhythms of the sun and the moon.*

In our modern world, engineered conveniences have allowed us to break free from our dependence on natural light. But these conveniences have also weakened our link to the daily rhythms that can help give order to our lives.

Days of Wonder, Nights of Peace draws upon our ancient tradition of morning and evening prayers to help us give our children a sense of ordered, daily rhythm at those moments that are part of each and every day—waking up and going to bed. The songs included here, two for morning and two for evening, have been written with families in mind. Their simple yet powerful themes of thankfulness, everyday miracles, creation, and protection can help us teach our children to infuse with meaning even the routine parts of each day.

We hope that these songs, and the rituals you choose to develop around them, will allow you and your children to celebrate daily moments together in a way that is uniquely Jewish. For when our days have rhythm and meaning, when we experience joy and express gratitude for the miracle that is our world, then we can certainly begin each new day with wonder, and enter each night in peace.

L'shalom, Mah Tovu   לְשָׁלוֹם, מַה טֹבוּ

FOR OUR CHILDREN:

Micah and Benjamin Chasen, Isa Zweiback,
and Benjamin Brodsky

HOW TO USE THIS CD

Start with the Songs. Bedtime is a natural time for daily rituals. The evening songs on this CD can easily be added to an existing bedtime routine, or used to establish a new one. And while your mornings may feel too harried for more than the usual scramble for shoes and socks, the morning songs here can provide a cheerful distraction while you help your youngster dress and get ready for the day. Lyrics are included to help you and your children sing along.

Make Them a Habit. The comfort of any ritual lies in its repetition. Daily routines help children feel more secure by teaching them what to expect in a world that is still new to them. An infant put to bed nightly to the peaceful strains of *Hashkiveinu* learns it is time for sleep. A three-year-old hearing *Round and Round* in the car each morning knows nursery school is just around the corner. Just choose a special time each day, and press play!

Make Them Your Own. The dearest rituals are often those we create ourselves. Ideas for developing family prayers are included in this book. And don't forget the fun—games can be rituals too. Try the Israeli version of "This Little Piggy" on page 9, or the memory game on page 17.

A Special Note: *In Jewish tradition, days are counted from sundown to sundown. This CD begins with morning songs, however, and progresses to evening ones for purely practical reasons. Feel free to use them in any order you wish.*

בֹּקֶר טוֹב

BOKER TOV

Good Morning: Rise Up to Life.

Each day begins with a miracle: sunrise. Our planet is in the perfect spot. The amount of warmth and light from the sun allows life not just to exist, but to flourish. We recognize the wonder of this balance, the marvel of life on Earth, and we give thanks to God, Creator of All Life.

The Torah tells of Abraham rising in the morning to go to the place where he had stood before God (Gen. 19:27). This act has been interpreted in the Talmud as the beginning of the ancient tradition of morning prayer that has carried through the ages. The patriarchs Isaac and Jacob are credited with instituting the afternoon and evening prayer services.

As part of this tradition, it is considered a mitzvah to teach even our youngest children to begin and end each day with the Sh'ma. Maimonides wrote that we should also teach them this verse from Deuteronomy:

תּוֹרָה צִוָּה לָנוּ מֹשֶׁה, מוֹרָשָׁה קְהִלַּת יַעֲקֹב.

Torah tziva lanu Moshe, morasha kehillat Ya'akov.

The Torah handed down from Moses is the inheritance of the community of Jacob (Deut. 33:4).

We teach our children to rise up and welcome the day by greeting God in prayer. We can greet each other in Hebrew with the phrase Boker tov! (Good morning!) The traditional answer is Boker or! (A morning of light!)

3

מוֹדֶה אֲנִי
MODEH ANI

Wake up you sleepyhead.
Open your eyes and get out of bed.
The sun is up and it's a beautiful day
There's so much to do, let's go out and play.

CHORUS:

מוֹדֶה (מוֹדָה) אֲנִי לְפָנֶיךָ, מֶלֶךְ חַי וְקַיָּם

Modeh ani l'fanechah melech ḥai v'kayam

שֶׁהֶחֱזַרְתָּ בִּי נִשְׁמָתִי בְּחֶמְלָה, רַבָּה אֱמוּנָתֶךָ.

She'heḥezarta bi nishmati beḥemlah rabbah emunatecha.

But before we get up to wash and dress,
Before we brush our teeth you know we've got to bless,
And say, "Thank You God for taking care of my soul.
You return it to me—yeah You make me whole."

CHORUS

I thank You God,
I just know You're out there.
You give my soul back to me,
Now I'm gonna make today all that it can be.

Late last night before we went to sleep
We prayed to God for our souls to keep.
Now that we're up and feeling fine,
We say, "Thank You" to God one more time.

(REPEAT CHORUS TWICE)

KAVANOT כַּוָּנוֹת

REFLECTIONS

In Jewish tradition, *Modeh Ani* is the first prayer uttered upon awakening in the morning. We begin a new day by thanking God for restoring the gift of life to us. On the CD, Josh, Ken, and Steve sing the word *modeh* because they are all men, and this is the masculine form; women and girls say *modah*.

מוֹדֶה (מוֹדָה) אֲנִי לְפָנֶיךָ, מֶלֶךְ חַי וְקַיָּם

Modeh (modah) ani l'fanechah melech hai v'kayam

I am thankful to You, Eternal Ruler,

שֶׁהֶחֱזַרְתָּ בִּי נִשְׁמָתִי בְּחֶמְלָה, רַבָּה אֱמוּנָתֶךָ.

She'hehezarta bi nishmati behemlah rabbah emunatecha.

For returning my soul to me in compassion.
Your faithfulness is abundant beyond measure.

The message of the abundance of God's faithfulness is taken from Lam. 3:22–23. The Jewish people were in great pain over the destruction of the First Temple, but were comforted by the belief that the grace of God continues in spite of everything. God's mercy and compassion are renewed for us each morning. Thus *Modeh Ani* is a prayer of profound hope and optimism: Today is a new day. We are alive. We have another chance.

ROUND AND ROUND

CHORUS:
**Every morning the sun comes up,
And every evening the sun goes down.
It's a beautiful thing the way it all works together,
And the world goes round and round.**

**The minutes and the hours and the days pass by,
Months turn to years but I don't know why.
God makes it all happen right before our eyes,
And the world goes round and round.**

The Torah tells the story of the days of creation.
God worked hard for six and then took a vacation.
The moon and the stars were quite a sensation,
And the world goes round and round.

The beasts of the ground and the birds of the air,
Some with feathers and some with hair.
And then woman and man, well they were quite a pair,
And the world goes round and round . . . *CHORUS*

Spring leads to summer and then comes fall,
Followed by winter, but that's not all.
When the snow comes down we're gonna have a ball,
And the world goes round and round.

Before you know it, it's the first day of spring.
The flowers will bloom and the birds will sing.
It's really quite amazing, this seasons thing,
And the world goes round and round . . . *CHORUS*

The wonder of the universe is hidden everywhere,
If we only take the time to look around.

The million tiny miracles that happen every moment,
Are presents from the Holy One just waiting to be found.
CHORUS

כַּוָּנוֹת KAVANOT
REFLECTIONS

"Round and Round" is based on a prayer called *Yotzeir Or*, the first of three prayers that surround the recitation of the *Sh'ma* in every morning service. This traditional prayer thanks God for the miracle of creation:

בָּרוּךְ אַתָּה יְיָ, אֱלֹהֵינוּ מֶלֶךְ הָעוֹלָם

Baruch Atah Adonai, Eloheinu melech ha'olam

Blessed are You Adonai, Ruler of the Universe

יוֹצֵר אוֹר וּבוֹרֵא חֹשֶׁךְ עֹשֶׂה שָׁלוֹם וּבוֹרֵא אֶת-הַכֹּל.

Yotzeir or uvorey hoshech oseh shalom uvorey et hakol.

Who fashions light and darkness, who makes peace and is the Creator of everything.

This prayer has its roots in Isa. 45:7, in which God is said to have created not only light, darkness, and peace, but also evil or trouble. Although rabbis changed the wording long ago, it remains part of Jewish tradition to acknowledge that there is good and bad in everything. In fact, everyone (our children included!) is considered to have *yetzer tov* (an inclination for good) and *yetzer hara* (an inclination for trouble), both of which are essential to life. We are reminded that our most difficult traits can also be our greatest strengths.

CREATE A FAMILY MORNING PRAYER

You and your child can finish the following sentences to create your own morning prayer. The idea banks provide suggestions, but feel free to come up with your own. And you can change your prayer as often as you like.

> **Adonai, our God and God of all generations, God of Abraham and Sarah, Isaac and Rebekah, Jacob, Rachel, and Leah, God of** _____ (include names of grandparents, siblings, and friends),

We thank You for giving us another day.

On this new day, help us to _____.

> **IDEA BANK:** be good, help others, enjoy Your world, take care of Your world, treat others as we would like to be treated

May this day be filled with _____.

> **IDEA BANK:** happiness, sunshine, fun

(Optional for when a loved one is ill:
May _____ feel better and may today be a good day for her/him.)

We will say thanks to You, God, by doing our best to make the world a better place today.

Amen.

MORNING RITUALS FOR EVERY DAY

Some of us wake up ready and eager to face the day. Others of us take a little longer to get the sleep out of our eyes. A morning song and a waking up game can help coax a sleepy head out of bed, or keep a squirming toddler on the changing table!

GRANDMA COOKED PORRIDGE

Do you enjoy playing with baby's toes but feel uncomfortable sending little piggies to market? This Israeli version lends Jewish flair to an old secular standard.

סַבְתָּא בִּישְׁלָה דַּיְסָה

נָתְנָה לְאַבָּא, נָתְנָה לְאִמָּא

נָתְנָה לְ____, נָתְנָה לְ____.

וְרַק לְ____ לֹא נִשְׁאַר!

הָלַךְ, הָלַךְ, הָלַךְ. . .

Safta bishlah daisah.
Natnah l'Abba, natnah l'Ima,
Natnah l'_____, natnah l'_____.
V'rak l'_____ lo nish'ar!
Halach, halach, halach . . . .

Grandma cooked some porridge.
She gave a little to Daddy, she gave a little to Mommy,
She gave a little to _____ (name another person),
She gave a little to _____ (name another person).
And only _____ (child's name) didn't get enough!
So (child's name or he/she) went and went and went . . .

(Insert tickling here!)

CREATION RHYMING GAME

The first player names something God made. The second player tries to think of something that rhymes with whatever the first player named. (Silly answers make this especially fun.)

Example:

God made seas. God made _____.
God made camels. God made _____.

If your children are young, let them say the first word, and you find a rhyme; older children may enjoy the challenge of trying to make the rhyme themselves.

You can also play an ABC acrostic game, in keeping with the Hebrew acrostic that can be found in the *Yotzeir Or* prayer. See if you and your child can think of a creation for every letter of the alphabet!

GOD MADE MY BODY GAME

Very young children may not be ready for rhyming, but they might enjoy this: Point to different parts of your child's body as you recite the name of each part. After two or three, leave the name out, and let your child fill in the blank.

Example:

God made these eyes, God made this nose, God made these fingers, God made these _____ (point to toes).

To add a little silliness, say the wrong thing. Your child will delight in correcting you!

לַיְלָה טוֹב

LAILAH TOV
Good night: Lie Down in Peace

Among ancient cultures, night was frightening and sleep itself mysterious. The sages of the Talmud thought that the soul departed the body during the night, only to be returned, God willing, in the morning. The Midrash—a rabbinic interpretation and explanation of the Bible—imagines what Adam's first night on earth must have felt like:

> When Adam saw the sun set for the first time, he was frightened by the darkness. He was afraid that the sun would never rise again. God decided to comfort Adam by teaching him to create fire. When Adam saw the light and felt the warmth of the fire, he was no longer scared. In gratitude, he offered a blessing of thanks for God's love and concern that guided him through the night.
>
> — adapted from Genesis Rabbah 12:6

Even now, night can be a time of fear, especially for children. Nightlights, stories, and security blankets can help dispel that fear. And, just as they did in ancient times, rituals can help comfort us when we lie down and cheer us when we rise up.

The end of the day is the perfect time to thank God for the world we live in and the people who are special to us. Then, as we face the night and get ready for sleep, we ask God to shelter us, and keep us safe until morning.

THANK YOU GOD

Thank You God—for giving me this day.
Thank You God—for the good You've brought my way.
For my breath, for my life,
For my soul that's in Your care.
I thank You, God, for all the gifts You share.

Thank You God—for the mountains and the seas.
Thank You God—for the birds and the trees.
For the grass, for the air,
For the water and the ground.
I thank You for the wonders all around.

There are so many miracles
I take for granted every day.
But my eyes are open now. I see them all.
So I've got to say . . .

Thank You God—(add your own blessing)
Thank You God—(add another)
I thank You for the blessings that are mine.

Thank You God—for my family.
Thank You God—for the love they shine on me.
For my teachers, for my friends,
For those I never got to know.
I thank You, God, for all who've helped me grow.

For the mountains and the seas; for the birds and the trees.
For my teachers and my friends;
For the love that never ends.
For my breath, for my life; for my soul that's in Your care.
I thank You, God, for all the gifts you share.

KAVANOT כַּוָּנוֹת
REFLECTIONS

"Thank You God" is based on the *Modim* prayer, which begins:

מוֹדִים אֲנַחְנוּ לָךְ, שָׁאַתָּה הוּא יְיָ אֱלֹהֵינוּ
וֵאלֹהֵי אֲבוֹתֵינוּ וְאִמּוֹתֵינוּ לְעוֹלָם וָעֶד.

*Modim anaḥnu lach, sha'atah hu Adonai Eloheinu
veilohei avoteinu v'imoteinu l'olam va'ed.*

We gratefully acknowledge that You are Adonai,
our God and God of our ancestors forever
and ever.

In this prayer, we declare our thanks to God for our lives
and souls, and for the everyday miracles we encounter
that remind us of God's presence. Though it may some-
times be hard to feel thankful, given the many problems
we see around us, our tradition constantly refocuses us on
the good by reminding us to offer words of praise.

Modim is one of the components of the *Amidah*, the cen-
tral part of all three daily services. It is one of the oldest
pieces of liturgy in Jewish tradition. The lyrics of this song
contain the concluding blessing from the prayer itself:

בָּרוּךְ אַתָּה יְיָ, הַטּוֹב שִׁמְךָ וּלְךָ נָאֶה לְהוֹדוֹת.

*Baruch Atah Adonai, ha'tov shimcha ul'cha
naeh l'hodot.*

Blessed are You, Adonai. Your name is
good, and it is fitting to give You thanks.

As we sing this song with our children we show them the
importance of recognizing God's role in the world, and
expressing gratitude to God for all the good things that
surround us.

HASHKIVEINU

הַשְׁכִּיבֵנוּ יְיָ אֱלֹהֵינוּ לְשָׁלוֹם, לְשָׁלוֹם

Hashkiveinu Adonai Eloheinu l'shalom, l'shalom

וְהַעֲמִידֵנוּ מַלְכֵּנוּ לְחַיִּים.

V'ha'amideinu malkeinu l'ḥayyim.

וּפְרוֹשׂ עָלֵינוּ סֻכַּת שְׁלוֹמֶךָ,

U'fros aleinu sukkat sh'lomecha, (2x)

אָמֵן

Amen

שְׁמַע יִשְׂרָאֵל יְיָ אֱלֹהֵינוּ, יְיָ אֶחָד.

Sh'ma Yisrael Adonai Eloheinu, Adonai eḥad. (2x)

בָּרוּךְ שֵׁם כְּבוֹד מַלְכוּתוֹ לְעוֹלָם וָעֶד.

Baruch sheim k'vod, malchuto, l'olam va'ed. (2x)

(repeat first stanza)

Shelter us beneath Thy wings, O Adonai.
Guard us from all harmful things, O Adonai.
Keep us safe throughout the night,
'Til we wake with morning's light.
Teach us, God, wrong from right. Amen.

Amen (repeat)

KAVANOT כַּוָּנוֹת
REFLECTIONS

Like bookends to our day, the *Sh'ma* is recited each morning and evening. In the morning service, it is surrounded by three prayers; in the evening service, two prayers precede the *Sh'ma* and two follow it. The gentle and lovely *Hashkiveinu* is the last of these prayers. It is also recited as part of the bedtime *Sh'ma*, and it captures the nighttime mood: Let us go to bed peacefully, but remember to get us up again. And, in both the sleeping and the waking, we seek the shelter of God's peace in our lives.

הַשְׁכִּיבֵנוּ יְיָ אֱלֹהֵינוּ לְשָׁלוֹם,

Hashkiveinu Adonai Eloheinu l'shalom
Cause us to lie down, Adonai our God,
in peace

וְהַעֲמִידֵנוּ מַלְכֵּנוּ לְחַיִּים.

V'ha'amideinu malkeinu l'hayyim.
And let us rise up again, our Ruler, to life.

וּפְרוֹשׂ עָלֵינוּ סֻכַּת שְׁלוֹמֶךָ, אָמֵן.

U'fros aleinu sukkat sh'lomecha, amen.
Spread over us the shelter of Your peace,
amen.

שְׁמַע יִשְׂרָאֵל יְיָ אֱלֹהֵינוּ, יְיָ אֶחָד.

Sh'ma Yisrael Adonai Eloheinu, Adonai ehad.
Hear, O Israel, Adonai our God, Adonai
is One.

בָּרוּךְ שֵׁם כְּבוֹד מַלְכוּתוֹ לְעוֹלָם וָעֶד.

Baruch sheim k'vod, malchuto, l'olam va'ed.
Blessed is our Ruler's glorious sovereignty
for ever and ever.

CREATE A FAMILY BEDTIME PRAYER

You and your child can finish the following sentences to create your own nighttime prayer. The idea banks are simply suggestions.

Adonai, our God and God of all generations, God of Abraham and Sarah, Isaac and Rebekah, Jacob, Rachel, and Leah,
God of _____ (include the names of grandparents, siblings, and friends),

Bless our family, loved ones and all humanity with_____.

> **IDEA BANK:** love, kindness, shalom (peace), freedom, goodness

Thank You, God, for filling this day with_____.

> **IDEA BANK:** happiness, fun, sunshine, good weather, hope, friends

(Optional for when a loved one is ill:
May _____ feel better and sleep peacefully tonight.)

Keep us safe throughout the night and make our dreams sweet.

Amen.

BEDTIME RITUALS FOR EVERY DAY

Taking baths, brushing teeth, getting that last glass of water: These are the things our children do each night before bed. We can add special family rituals to create a moment that goes beyond the duty of nightly chores to invest each day with meaning and with a feeling that is uniquely Jewish. Playing the nighttime songs on this CD, reading stories together, and saying a special bedtime prayer are all natural ways to bring peacefulness to the end of each day. Quiet games are also a nice way to make the transition from daytime to bedtime.

THANK YOU ACROSTIC

Take turns with your child naming things you are thankful for, using the letters in the words "Thank You". Or use your child's name. Answers can be serious, but children love silly answers, too.

MEMORY GAME
(Great for any number of players.)

The first player begins: Today I was thankful for _____.
The second player continues, repeating the first player's choice, and adding another. The third player repeats the first two, and names a third, and the game continues until there are too many things to recall. How many things can YOU remember? (And don't forget, silly answers can add to the fun!)

Example:

1st person: Today I was thankful for sunshine.

2nd person: Today I was thankful for sunshine and sprinklers.

3rd person: Today I was thankful for sunshine and sprinklers and Popsicles.

1st person again: Today I was thankful for sunshine and sprinklers and Popsicles and Grandma. . . etc.

GOOD NIGHT, SLEEP TIGHT

By saying good night to the things around them, young children can discover a calming way to get ready for sleep, while learning about their world. This simple poem can be changed for all manner of special people or belongings. If you want to add some Hebrew, a short list of common words is also included.

This is my bear.

Time for bed, bear.

Good night, sleep tight.

I'll see you again in the morning.

IDEAS:

Bear/dov:	דֹּב
Mommy/Ima:	אִמָּא
Daddy/Abba:	אַבָּא
Blanket/s'micha:	שְׂמִיכָה
Doll/bubah:	בֻּבָּה
Lamp/menorah:	מְנוֹרָה
Toy/tza'atzua:	צַעֲצוּעַ
Pillow/kar:	כַּר